Ovation Face

Erotic poetry by
S.A. Harper

Word Oyster Press

Other work by S.A. Harper

Poetry
All These Pronouns Jump Bones
Rapture in Arrears

Short Stories
Feeding the Two-Backed Beast
Ephemeral
Tweed & Other Stories

Contents

"You can tell it's a poem because it's swimming in a little gel pack of white space. That shows it's a poem."

— Nicholson Baker

"Feel free to cover your eyes at anything that might upset you."

— Annie Sprinkle

Paean

I hear Matilda's nooner nipples sing
their rosy radiance of the recently tongued
(or bitten and tweaked, who's to say?),

their voices burning through the white top sheet,
making declarations, explicating something,
refusing to hush or shrink away without first

showing off their colors of a sailor's sunrise,
his Beamer barely having turned the corner,
the screen door still settling from being slammed.

The plumber gives the mailman some side-eye
because the whole block knows Matilda's well-fucked.
Seems redundant now for her pussy to start scatting,

riffing like a horn that's already in Dilltown,
improvising the fricatives, the plosives,
performing the tempo like a one-woman show.

Carnose

Here we are with our scratched flesh,
the bitten nipples, pink and raw,
tongue that's tickled buttholes dizzy,

expecting ventriloquist answers
from the flesh, the puckered flesh
squeezing shut, daring to open.

It's the flesh of it, the skin and blood
(but not the bone, not the
raccoon's curved baculum

when it might come in handy…
then again, you can't break
what you don't have),

swelling flesh, sleek and ready to enter,
or wet and willing to surround, both
all in for the moment, putting flesh inside,

maybe no longer having an inside
that isn't already filled with skin and flesh,
maybe even a finger up the backside

(yep, there's the bones in boning,
the phalanges and their come-hither curl),
skin eaten whole, flesh swallowed whole,

stretched or stretching, head just in
or the unexpurgated disappearance complete,
pimple freckle wrinkle flesh, all the ways

skin slides on skin, sticks to skin,
how hands can pull two thighs apart
and find that mouth's still not speaking,

can pinch her flesh together, left and right,
get a good grip and give it all a shake —
the outer, the inner, the coxswain in the boat.

It's the flesh, always the flesh spurting
pearls of fact, confessing clear truths
about what flesh is, what flesh is —

the tissue paper on the lingerie,
the burlap drawstring keeping shut
these shiny/nasty bags of meat.

declination

we became polar opposites last night:
my fretful north to your cynical south,
your obverse in inverted reverse,

our four feet dancing some sluggish samba
near each other's shrugged shoulders,
learning what it is to read a compass blind,

aligned and levitating along some lines of force,
trying to complete a circle, many circles,
their geographical coincidence the paths

along which our displaced spirits soar,
all these bright, imagined birds flying home with
their tiny bits of iron in their tiny little heads,

us rotating in compromise, realigned on pillows,
me tinkering with your astrolabe, you my Brunton,
sleeping spent and happy on a bed of stars.

Cold Snap

Ah, there it is.

The cold air's arrived,
and I know now I won't
see your bare toes wiggle
'til late May, maybe June.

That's months of hearing your socks
shuffle down the hallway, feel them
sneak under my leg as we watch TV,
or (socks changed) see them slip into bed.

Warm feet matter most. The rest is gravy.
As long as your feet are toasty, I've seen
you walk around in a t-shirt, nips out,
ass textured in goosebumps, happy as a clam.

Last night, you saw me work with that:
your ankles tied to the headboard, fuzzy feet
over your shoulders, toes curling in their cocoons,
me pulling open a second source of heat…

Ah, and there it is.

Haiku I

you hover above
nipples dancing on my lips
lazy pirouettes

~

Larger dinosaurs
had extra brains for their tails.
My cock? No such luck.

~

nibble 'round the pit
savor sweet her freestone peach
wet face clinging fast

~

the mood strikes mid-show
we hit Pause and go at it
a bedroom too far

worshipped at her toes
she wants his attentions
a few feet higher

~

Stuffed into your mouth:
pink cotton bikini brief.
What's that you're saying?

~

That barn from our youth?
Slow rot and creeping collapse;
no more handjobs there.

~

silly silly boy
tries hard to hit my cervix
this isn't hentai

Raincheck

We should get an A for effort.
We've barely moved for five minutes,
    faces pressed against each other,
    quietly talking into each other's mouths,
    sentences ending in slight kisses,
trying to maintain as long as possible
what it is we have, this doomed interval,
    no taking it back, unable to undo
    depth and volume we lose bit by bit,
    delaying the moment until you're empty,
and the wet worm of me has wriggled out —
so cold, cold, not-inside-you cold.

Initial Soundings

That girl I wanted to make flow like a river?
She said I did and said, "You wanna see?"
before putting my hand between her legs.

But every time we made out that fall,
she wore thick cords or denim jeans.
Truth is, I couldn't feel a damp thing.

Likewise, she knew where it stood with me,
could make out the shape and size of desire
no matter where in my pants I pinned it,

but with the indisputable pressed against her,
she still couldn't feel the hard heat of my skin
or the pulse I knew she knew was there.

Well, that's being 15 for you.
That's being such "good kids"
that we didn't even think to unbutton.

We were still new from the store,
wrapped up with paper and twine.
We were matches locked up in Lucite,

dynamite one zipper pull from exploding,
one overlooked river lapping at the levee,
two blind doodles crowing in the dark.

Less Reflection, More Compaction

I think my Nice Guy
thinks too much.

In bed, in the throes,
in all the sweaty moments,
these kind considerations
I've never asked for
pretty much kill me
every time.

He doesn't want to crush me,
but it's his weight I want.

I want all of his weight
pressing me down
until I've made
a lasting impression
in the memory foam.
I want to be fucked flat —
compacted, compressed,
squished until I have no voice,
allowed only shallow breaths,
in and out in thimbles full,
gasping and breathing breathless.

When we're making
the Beast with Two Backs,
I want him to break mine.

Instead, he hovers above me,
propped up on wobbly arms
even after, even after, even
when he should collapse
and pin me to the mat,
passed out before the count,
down for it, towel thrown in.

For the love of Mike, I tell you.
I want to be almost suffocated,
not admired until almost dying.

Morning Glory

Your sunrise tent pole is not my handiwork.
It existed before I began to examine,
before I first poked at its prominence,
before I pulled back the sheet to see.

You always claim you wake so hard
from your nightly soft-as-pillows dreams
without anyone's guest appearance, nameless
inspirations here and gone like a caress.

I don't care if it's not always me... or anyone.
Why it happens doesn't matter as much as what —
the bobbing explicitness of your autonomic desire.
I watch this show for the plaything, not the plot.

Even when you're asleep,
how fervently it jumps to my hand!

Bumble Handed Me a Lemon

To whom much was given, much was expected.
But I handed you free rein, and you cantered in my corral.
I gave you keys to my well-stocked cupboard
(my cookie jar, my lockbox, my stash of bonbons,
and the WiFi password to my Cave of Winds),
and you walked past the goodies, settled for saltines.

I gave you two days of anything goes,
and you shot your bolt by noon, Day One.

Was I wrong to expect a lover with range,
one who sees the impact-play potential
in a years-old wooden spoon or a rolled-up magazine,
one who doesn't need reminding about the varieties of touch,
how sometimes a fondle is inferior to a slap,
how even a nasty bite can be as good as a nibble?

As a missionary, you couldn't even
convert my willing knees apart.

You really were a waste of wine and hummus,
of bathing and shaving and cleaning my toys.
You left all my anticipations unfulfilled,
my couch cushions still in place, nothing broken,
my lubricants untested, no messes made,
no body count, no stories. Not a single bruise.

You brought one napkin to a feast.
You sat at my banquet with a spork.

The Other Shoe is a Dildo

You dangle from an exposed beam
    (one of our realtor's cute details
    I found purely aesthetic until now),
your wrists aching, thighs quaking
    (rope 42 cents per foot from Lowes,
    knots practiced each night on the sly),
trying so hard to maintain, to be good,
to keep inside you this object, this thing
that gravity rightly insists must fall out
and which I've warned you
    must
        never
            ever
                drop.
You clutch at it, conjuring Kegels. It holds.
You clench, then quiver. You falter. It moves.
You panic, squeeze your knees together, almost
able to regain control until your toes tire.
Adjust your weight? It slips. One inch lost.

Your exasperation and your desire to be done
are now tangled together like a ball of snakes.

I cannot lower the beam or raise the floor.
But I can shove it back up, back to the start,
kiss you until you'd rather blush than giggle,
let you try to push the boulder up the hill,
inexorable failure its own reward.

to those who wait

hold the pepper and the salt.
hold the condiments, the gravy,
the glass-rim lemon wedges,
the server's grated cheese.

hold the line, and hold things steady.
hold expectations, recurring dreams,
the maxed-out heart, the crow's feet,
the disappointment, the rapture.

hold your shins and pull them back.
hold your breath, await the nuzzling nose,
the rapid flick, the final full-flat lap,
the fingers, the swirl, the stab.

Unclaimed Benefits

In the eye of this beholder,
the vitreous humor is clear
but can't tell a joke worth shit.
It's all about the numbers for that one.

I'd never drawn you before today.
But today, you're one pot gummy bold enough
to tell me, friends or not, it's weird that I haven't.
I offer you a bath sheet and get my supplies.

I can't tell if you're bare-assed beneath the towel.
But you are barefoot, and that should count
for something. You sit on the table. I sit on a chair.
The three-quarters pose is one-quarter unsettling.

It seems your back is dusted with freckles.
(I always knew you had a back. The shoulders
I've seen with their spots popping out in summer,
the topmost arcs of your shoulder blades,

and the bump of your spine at your neck
when you put your hair up with a pencil.)
Maybe I can't draw your back with just charcoal.
I can get the shape but can't grasp the volume.

I decide to approach you as separate parts.
I can draw a foot or a wrist on its own.
A shin bone can become a straight line
from the right angle, even stoned as this.

When I draw, I second-guess what I see
and dream up what I can't. In that world,
I've witnessed a butterfly tattoo fly up
from your calf to your thigh like ascending faith

and a hundred more fly down in revelation.
My fingers are messy. My mind's messier.
The towel droops. A nipple springs free.
I can't erase what I won't unsee.

the big reveal

protected unplucked the lady's slipper
peeps pink from moss beneath the pine,
quivers in summer sunlight breeze,
a commoner's orchid, something
fortuitous to find, easy to expose,
obvious for those who know to look
and, looking most like what it is,
dares to give you a passing eyeful.

there's nothing to do but stare it down.
unbuckle, unzip, drop your shorts, and squat.
give it an eyeful back. make it blink.
see if game recognizes game.

burn the witch

above the bed, above your head,
a necklace of knuckles strung
with catgut rattling on the wall

of an empty cabin, doors barred
to unbelievers, casting your spells,
riding your broomstick, high on

self-immolation, the whimsy of fire
you light in yourself, the familiar
three fingers in constant flight,

thinking of no one special, no one
who couldn't have three fingers or
a cock, tits, tongue, blazing juicy slit

that laughs long at their tribunals,
the inquisitor, the thumbscrew, the rack.
they can't kindle what's already consumed.

Haiku II

Watch her twirl her skirt!
This carnival ride reveals
all the fine fannies.

~

Be still little fruit
or you'll come like a kumquat:
bitten and you burst.

~

resource underused
a bed big enough for three
should give that a go

~

pheromones so strong
vanilla behind each ear
won't fool anyone

your aspergillum
anoints my face with thick cum
true absolution

~

modest to a point
he enjoys her last coy smile
then her panties fall

~

July 4th handjob
passing time as dusk deepens
can't miss the fireworks

~

all access granted
you choose your way carefully
in through the out door

COVID Quarantine (Week 5)

Too many hours each day spent thinking of masks —
the size of things we cannot see and holes in everything.
At least we no longer bleach our groceries. There's that.
You tell me you're making great strides with sourdough.

In this prolonged separation, we bolster each other
with texts and sexts, quick calls, and late-night Zooms.
You have judged no nude too gratuitous to send.
In return, you've seen my butt with googly eyes.

It's likely neither of us will starve in our isolation.
There will be no atrophy, no loss of soul-weight,
no clothes or thoughts carelessly slipping from our bones,
no greetings or metaphors forgotten. I bet we'll be OK.

But I still want you here, gasping for air on this bed,
only breathless because you like it from behind.
When the lockdown's lifted, think of what we'll do
when — at last — they wheel the ventilators away.

popsicle

pursed puckered pleased:
precisely applied lipstick
less perilous to prod than peruse.

red double peaks of her upper lip
pulled down tight in a sharp smile,
arrow launched from Cupid's bow.

plucked string, purpose performed,
consummate culmination,
his crimson perimeter, a cock tale told.

Mattress Topper

I've turned over, and there's no turning back,
flat and getting flatter, belly down
as you work your cock's blunt head
between my ass cheeks, between my legs,

getting your prick slick with my only effort,
working until you find the spot in the groove,
then pushing in, me still not moving,
breasts becoming one with the sheet.

I could make this easier, I know.
I could raise my ass, flex, pivot,
get up on all fours and let you
grab my hips and pull.

But I won't. I barely spread an inch for you,
make you put your knees outside mine,
make what's tight in me tighter, harder
for you to move, making you bend inside me

until you're angry without knowing it,
pounding away, thrusts ending in thuds,
the impact, action, and reaction ripples
spreading from my ass to my chest.

I turn my head to the side, cheek down
and cool against our 400 thread count,
flat at first and now fucked flatter,
two dimensions, a hole in the mattress.

Mid-June, Idyll with IPA

A marsh wren chitters at no one special,
but the catbird's call seems meant for us:
"Go! Go!" as if we aren't already at the water.

Two frogs' throaty thrums somehow merge
and become a chorus for crickets' lulling buzz,
dry air no longer smelling sweet of May.

We sit unbuckled on a lakeside ledge
having each had two beers and a needed pee,
fingers now fiddling in each other's shorts,

finding comfort in unhurried exploration,
rolling the shiny pebbles, plucking the reeds
until fish stop to see what the hell's the matter.

chicory

two buttery breasts
made powder white
by beignet sugar drifts,

slow-motion avalanche,
casual chaos without care,
nothing ventured except a sneeze.

cat content, you wait and chew
as first my tongue, then his,
make this cleanup quick.

binge watch

one episode too many
of "Is That Cake?"
and pants are coming off.

cuz no matter how much
hot yoga the boy does,
it's not gonna blow itself.

yes, he'll reciprocate.
and find my center sweet.
in certain light, everything's cake,

and fondant can fool all takers.
the thing about a piping bag.
is knowing where to squeeze.

Blind Man / Elephant

You ask what it feels like when I come.
Here is this most basic human thing —
so standard, so universal, so common —
and yet I cannot begin to describe for you
whether (for me) it's more like falling,

melting, or finding all my liquids turned to ice,
unable to recognize what approaches —
a tingle, a tickle, something rushing somewhere,
rockfall rumble, machine gun scatter,
the white flag of surrender, a loss of control.

In coming, I make peace with the impossible:
my map's borders flung open, their line style dashed,
no longer separate, at one with my surroundings,
having passed unmussed through the needle's eye
and emptied myself of another everyday miracle.

Popper

You can keep your fox tails
and your horse tails.

And it's a hard pass for me
on cute white cottontails

and the pink corkscrews
of piggly-wiggly tails.

Your butt plug should have
a train of crepe paper streamers.

I want to hear them rustling
as you walk down our hallway.

I want to see all those festive
colors spilling from your ass

like a birthday party.

Flood Stage

Don't bring me an ambivalent sprinkle,
no drawn-out drizzle, no ephemeral gentle rain
that ends as it starts, flowers barely damp.

We've petted 'til you see how hard I thunder,
played fore until our lips are tender and bruised.
I can't dowse in your grasslands any longer.

If this is to be, then show me a surge, a deluge.
Let me drown with your riverbanks overflowing,
carried down, drenched, sodden in excess.

Soaked.

Spotlight

Summer solstice flashlight tag — and I'm It.
So, I seek the shapes in darkness deepening,
hear heavy footfall, running sneakers,

our friends getting farther away, lurking
several houses down the street, almost
to the corner and far from home.

Now, a silhouette behind the neighbor's shed:
someone I'd hoped would only half-heartedly hide,
someone waving what could be a bra.

Steady, I shine my beam,
and your shirt drops
to the ground.

Tag.

Burial / Resurrection

There's grass beneath my fingers, an acorn cap,
half-empty oaks above me framing the sky,
as you in your cable knit sweater

rake leaves on top of me until I'm covered,
so resolved, so thorough, raking until I vanish
into the deepening, making me the secret center

of a leaf pile, making me the gooey marshmallow
in the middle of a cupcake hidden in plain view
in the large front yard of a small Ranch house

in the aging suburbs of an old city on an online map.
There must be a hundred other piles of leaves
in this neighborhood today, but not one has me.

I keep my eyes closed and listen as you rake nearby
or rake more distant leaves closer and onto the pile,
not heavy, but thicker, the thought weighing me down,

less light on my eyelids, the smell of how decay begins.
Then? No sound at all. Well, birds and cars. Someone
using a leaf blower. But to me, you've gone missing.

Waiting isn't easy. Waiting's never easy.
Have you left me here, or will you come running
and jump on our pile like a child, crush me

or dig me out like a forgotten treasure?
Or will you return with even more leaves,
making the pile taller and me less significant?

The leaves rustle, and a hand reaches into the pile to find
a breast to catch, my belly, my belt. It's you, and
I'm in autumn's grope box, too clothed for November,

unable to open my mouth for the leaves,
unable to open my eyes for the leaves,
buried crisp in the leaves, soon to be green again.

Haiku III

Skin hot from spanking,
I wait for his cool caress.
I'm complicated.

~

diddly-squat diddled
swelling something surfaces
give the sprout some love

~

spidey sense tingles
(except, really, it's my cock
and you're the villain)

~

one or sometimes two
how many fingers inside
hold your attention

I tried to paint her
("Focus! Shapes are only shapes!")
but my brush got hard.

～

beneath the table
vantage point between my legs
dropped fork forgotten

～

almost a reflex
how rubbing this leads to that
good girl rolls over

～

reluctantly licked
the virgin stifles a laugh
grins as insight looms

Kintsugi

My heart is mended with gold epoxy
and sometimes gleams like crinkled foil.
It's still shaped mostly like a heart.
You'll find it skips, but keeps good time.

Of course, there's always one break left
where unstopped the light pours through.
There's never enough time to fix everything,
and imperfection has a certain lived-in look.

That breach is your way in. That's how
you can shock me back to a steady beat.
Pierce me there. Jam two fingers deep inside
and feel for the reset button, ridgy but firm.

With your help, I bet I can make my own gold
and fuse your fingers still crooked inside,
no room left for light to leak, just you in the crack,
twisting where I'm torn, me shuddering back.

Groundhog, Complicit

Seasons never change
with a smile or stoic shrug
or a goodbye waved in resignation.
They whine. They linger.
They drag their heels,
ask for one more cup of tea,
then pull up their Insta and scroll.

Winter's outstayed her welcome.
She's still blowing hard all night,
and you and I wake to a kitchen floor
colder than any we had weeks ago
when the calendar was insisting
she was well within her rights.
Let's face it. I'm done.

Foreplay shouldn't require mittens.
I want to remove your clothes
out from under these blankets,
have you stand there naked
and willing to be touched by hands
that didn't need any other preparation
than lust to get themselves warm.

For fuck's sake, the goldfinches
have nearly gone all yellow.
Winter, let us be.

Milestones, Mr. Goldstone

We sat on the couch,
    drinking Maker's Mark
    from gas station glasses,
watching *Gypsy*
on a black-and-white TV
I'd bought at Gold Circle
and hauled to Dallas
for my summer job.

There's Louise
    as the front end of the cow.
And there's Louise
    learning to take off an opera glove
    and ignore her mom.

With commercials, the movie
was at least two short drinks long
and didn't roll credits until one.
You asked if you could sleep over.
Neither of us suggested the couch.

We didn't know it then,
but Mt. St. Helens would
erupt eight hours after I did.
Not the volcano's first time.
But it was mine.

"Stay still," you said. "Don't pull out.
Maybe it'll come back."

Like vaudeville.

Roswell Tackle & Feed

In the sweet languor of silver sedation,
she has visions of being properly filled —
with eggs, sperm, whole small beings swimming
like schools of shiny minnows inside her,
taking up space that yesterday was her space,
less a void than a potential somewhere.

"Is this like the space they come from?
Was their first swim in another me?"

Each day, she swells suspended and weightless,
feels the twitching of things like arms,
the kicks of what she imagines are knees,
the thrashing growing brood of her promise
racing to be born, to pour out of her
in a wave she trembles to imagine.

"How long has it been since I was taken?
Do I go home? Have I been home? Do I stay?"

One day, she wakes in a bed that seems like hers,
stares at the ceiling, wants to get up, knows
she should rest and gather her strength
before the next ones come, the bug-eyed men
with their probes and their appendages,
inviting her along, taking her again to breed.

Mummy/Gummy

Katie's eating
Haribo gummy snakes in bed.
She's very mindful
to take just one snake
from the bag at a time
and to finish chewing one
before taking another.
She's in no hurry.

"These are so good,"
she tells Kevin.
Kevin doesn't reply.

Sometimes, she tells him
which flavor she's having next.
Sometimes she dangles
the gummy snake
over his face so the slits
she's left for eyes can see
the gummy before
she pops it in her mouth.
Katie's wrapped him up
so tight in Saran Wrap
that Kevin can't do much
more than squiggle and blink.

Red? Raspberry.
White. Pineapple.

She taps it. It wobbles.
She tugs it. It stays.
The dildo's suction cup
seems to be holding
to the plastic wrap
across his chest.

Orange. Orange, of course.

"Stay still now."
She mounts him
and slowly
slowly
moves.

Yellow. Lemon.
Orange again.

couldn't wait

we leave blood on the beach —
red on swimsuits, red on towels,
red dripping on sparkling sand

as we walk reborn into the waves,
awash in sunlight, submerged in surf,
admitting nothing to seagulls.

there's no one here to see another trickle,
more of me, some more of you, mixed
so well even sharks will tip their fins.

Token Regrets

Sunless Cape Cod afternoon:
no swimming, no sailing in the bay,
just rain and a cheap box of wine.

We decide to play Sorry for oral.
We draw our cards and move.
I have one pawn home, then three.

You bump my last man back to Start.
Now I'm impatient for a resolution
beyond these gameboard safety zones.

Space by space, I've grown restless
to reach the end, to make you
apologize with your tongue.

Always Whale Rock

I'm perched on a glacial erratic
(which itself is perched on a hill),
a rock green like copper, maybe brass,
with its algae coat soft between my bare ass
and some rough, dark, Ontario diorite.

I'm doing my best to demonstrate for you
exactly what it takes for a boulder this size
to be moved, how all great things like us
get carried away and eventually come
when there's desire and a little persistence.

Distracted

I need to leave for work,
     but you may wrap me in chains.
I should make dinner,
     but you may bind me tight.

And while I consider breathing a necessity,
sometimes I enjoy the thought of you
wrapping your fingers around my throat
and making me gasp like a goldfish
that's leapt with abandon from its bowl.

Surely you see I must come before I desiccate,
before the moment passes, before the bowl goes dry,
me still waiting for you to say when.

Say when. (The chains.)
Say when. (Your hands.)
Say when. (My throat.)

When.

Haiku IV

The dune grass dips, bends.
Protected plovers skitter.
Pull up his trunks. Spit.

∼

"the boat house at nine"
how my cousin told me where
to watch her first time

∼

shared by two sisters,
a young man's summer teeters
on this double-dare

∼

two cocks one pussy
never dreamed they both would fit
get together boys

lips red from Red Hots
her cinnamon tongue dancing
spicy in my mouth

~

pushed down in soft snow
her ski suit's sorry access
a flaw in our plan

~

Emma once told me,
"Small breasts want attention, too,"
both her buds like beans.

~

you wait and whimper
balloon made ready to pop
begging for pin's prick

Back from the CSA

I want you on the kitchen table,
a cherry tomato in your belly button,
cilantro tucked beneath each breast.

I want to kiss you through green lettuce.
I want to slap your pussy with anise
and stick a radish between your cheeks.

I want to make you leek.

labor day on the farm

attention unsought,
the red fox suggesting,
    grinning proffers
    her keen teeth pearly,
assumes wrongly
that fowl like us
    easy marks for smiled
    seduction must be.

not clever enough by far,
she can't conceive
how nightly we,
    both bonny goose
    and gainly gander,
warm against the
    farmer's daughter
            sleep spent.

Defrosting for Legroom

You're more
than a little
hot to the touch.
The fan rotates.
My plan evolves.

I propose we crawl
into the freezer
and make love
on a bed
of frozen peas.

After that,
I'll rest my balls
in an ice cube tray.
You can put a kielbasa
between your legs
and think of Dijon.

You seem rightly
cool to the idea,
which isn't a bad thing.
Pull the door shut.
Out goes the light.

Gaze Held, Shakily

Tessa always seems to have a hair tie or two
hiding in the front pockets of her jeans.
Probably a "be prepared" sort of thing.
Reading, cooking, planting flowers…
all times I've seen her use them.
Then now, mid-blowjob, with
my spit-wet cock bobbing
in the space between us,
she gets out a red elastic
and puts her hair back,
perhaps for neatness
or maybe because
what's the point
of eye contact
if I can't see
her eyes
or she
see
mine?

High Score

tap dance.
tap a keg.
tap the brakes.
tap dat ass.

We train for this by tireless repetition.
What worked once should work again:
the clothes-still-on speed run,
the three-condom endurance match,
the importance of positions,
the target, the approach, the kill.

break your fast.
break the bank.
break it in.
break a heart.

We've been here before and mastered
more than one boss level.
We know how to use haptic feedback.
(I twitch. You shudder.
You squeeze. I respond.)
I can't count the loot boxes we've plundered.

jump the gun.
jump through hoops.
jump their bones.
jump for joy.

I've lost track of hours we've logged,
the tally of intended little deaths,
you lying in wait, dripping bullets,
and me pushing hard into the same ambush,
dying happy to respawn on the same hill,
living the refractory period of a penitent man.

Involuntary Hold

I've gone Bedlam to Bellevue, misjudged
and locked up again for far less offense
than flashing my freckled ass at strangers,

exposed, caught wanting your prick so bad
that I howled in Walmart out of turn,
made a peck of prudes' heads spin clean 'round,

them ashamed to recognize why I cried,
remembering but keeping their counsel, knowing
damned well I dripped with honesty, not hysteria,

wearing T-swizzle's Armani straightjacket
(who better for butt stuff than a tight end?),
looking for Aisle 4's markdowns and feel-ups.

You can't commit me for an unzipped zipper.
You shouldn't shock me for being shocking.
I was always this way until you made me worse.

Pantone Color of the Year

It's the damned digital decay, this loss of proof
as phones die, pre-cloud photos fleeting or flit.
There's little to show now of my gratis boob-flashes,
how my breasts have changed shape, how the color
of my nipples has made a most merry promenade
from their first mornings of callow coral,
to afternoons of pale purple-pink, and now —
of course — long evenings of my mother's brown,
me settled and content to watch skies part,
and see you come in from a pouring rain
to greet me (and often those nipples)
with your appreciative, colorblind kiss.

tempest

this is why you stoke these fires, this beacon
the promise of a kiss when I come into port,
your lodestar drifting above the horizon,
sextant's true north for ten passing ships,

not one that can bear witness but me,
not one first mate who sees the obvious,
each weary soul oblivious to a nipple slip
coyly peeking from ocean's blue blouse,

why I first set sail on inevitable voyages
alongside men scurvy won't have twice,
why I left one who once passed me on the shore,
her red hair tousled, wishing me good day,

smiling as if all first nights never end.
I'm marking myself safe from this storm,
moored between your thighs, riding it out,
held in the calm, tight in movement's lull.

that's when it came to me

tossed like rice at a bride, the stars
lie scattered on the empty pitch
canvas of another clear night sky.

there's only one car in the lot, and it's ours.
for now, I guess we own this hill, this view.
your arm brushes mine. yes, I know you're there.

you tell me which stars are planets.
for some, you name their moons.
you put my hand in your back pocket

and dare me to guess your mind.
I tell you I'll guess your weight
because I know that'll be easier.

but when you put your hand in my pocket,
I see there's clarity in back versus front
and belatedly decide to take that dare.

Errands

No one knows what she wears
beneath the yellow-orange skirt
fluttering in a stiff November wind.

Only ten more stops for her to make
before I'll return what I borrowed,
eight stops when she calls to complain,

four stops and she thinks she sees the end.
At two stops, she bends to tie her shoe,
her hem riding up in smiling concession.

Home again, she spins for me bare-assed,
falling in my arms, mouth soon stuffed
with white cotton. Wide eyes, muffled squeal.

subject and medium

it's flushed red, this your mottled mosaic:
ass cheeks fresh with near-miss blush,
carnation streaks and rose-red welts,
scarlet finger-splashes edged in carmine.

tears drying, you're curious to see our canvas.
perhaps photos to chronicle our collaboration?
stand there and face the wall. raise your skirt.
just one more thing... say "cheese."

look. do the shapes diverge from what you feel?
do your colors echo what you imagined?

Haiku V

I watch you watch me
slowly pull my lips apart
lady tiger door

~

no elephant trunk
what he has inside his pants
can't grab a peanut

~

So it comes to this:
my ankles on his shoulders,
as you watch apart.

~

It's not always so.
Tonight I find your seed sweet.
Come and give me more.

She rises, then drops,
all his thrusting turned passive.
"Still. You're my toy now."

~

Open window nights:
sometimes you hear your neighbors;
sometimes they hear you.

~

Thank goodness for rope!
What's the point of a feather
if you run away?

~

so firm it's tender
how considerate his grip
capitulation

Projectile Motion

Can't say I saw that coming!
Last night, you came so hard
you shot the plug across the room.

So much for boops, flairs, and flanges.
"Watch what you're doing," my grandma would say.
"You'll put someone's eye out!"

The glass plug traveled a parabolic path —
an arc just like an ideal physics problem softball —
from your butt to the throw rug, its unintended target.

Here's an idea. Let's reload and try again.
This time, forget about hitting the bullseye.
Tonight, we go for distance.

Suddenly, September

I miss the girl
content to watch
my cock do tricks,

who found delight seeing it
swell from nothingness,

who took pride in knowing
she could make it get big,
go off, deflate, and rise again,

so happy to do just that,
again and again.

I miss that girl almost
as much as I miss that
stupid young cock:

the one that still did tricks.

Nuts

The news has been
a real shit show.
So, I've been watching
these slimmed-down,
"Paleo Diet my ass"
February squirrels
chase each other
all morning —

one after one,
then two after one
or four playing tag
around the trees
or under Mike's parked SUV,
maybe planning a jump scare
from the wheel well.
Never saw that coming.

I know I'm wasting time,
but what's their deal?
All this running.
So much energy spent
not even looking for
one chilled acorn,
nevermind enough food
to break a fast.

Well, duh. Now I learn
this could be the week
when the girl squirrel
twitches her tail

at the guy squirrels
and they chase her
to hell and back
to make her say, "Ooo, Baby!"

That makes more sense.
Tag's fine sometimes,
but I know this is
exactly how I'd be
if you'd only walk by
and wave your
tail at me.

Stomata

Too entangled to walk straight,
we amble side-to-side, curling
between dark trees in soft fog,

content with simple solutions,
our hands in each other's coats,
avoiding all cold drizzle, colder wind.

Some pockets open front and back,
so we reach through for warmth within,
soon forgetting what it is to walk at all,

hands lost in the other's world,
sleeves halfway up our arms,
another inch and another farther in,

two coats made into one straitjacket,
neither of us willing to surrender,
both of us reaching for something

just beyond that button, that seam,
the next layer pulled up, a belt undone,
an elusive heart with a singular heat.

Loose Ends

Quietly this chair and I discuss the Marvel Universe,
not yet the focus of your attention, our turn delayed.
But we both know the final act's end game.

This is no one's first rodeo.

You untangle, wrap, sort pieces from short to long.
In lesser hands, a mess of ropes is considered sloppy —
a sign one doesn't care for their tools.

The chair reassures me you're a pro.

I sense progress, see fewer knots multiplied in mirrors,
allow myself to hope for their impending recreation.
I long for the itchy dents, the marks rope makes in skin.

The chair didn't choose this. But I did.

How will you bind me? Limb to chair or wrist to ankle?
With my knees apart, arms back, breasts out? These are
the tight embraces I long for and the buttons they push.

I tell the chair how I will make it holy.

Find a Better Offer

I've decided to spend tomorrow naked —
not wearing a stitch from head to toe,
every bob and bit uncovered, a free range chick.

You're OK to look at what I'm not hiding —
all my goose pimples and freeform freckles,
my stretch marks, my skin tags, my scars,

the missed strip of hair from last night's shave,
the birthmark that looks like Iceland in June,
innie or outie, hairy or porcelain plain.

You'll see how surprised my asshole looks,
the symmetry of my tits when I stand,
the asymmetry of my pussy when I spread.

All you have to do is write
a 500-word essay on what you see.
Admit it. It's a pretty good deal.

Flattery Will Get Your Nose Wet

Praise my pussy.
Approach it softly on your knees.
Don't spook it by looking it in the eye.

Commend my cunt.
Compliment its curved cuneiform,
its cascades of clever curlies.

Laud my labia and venerate my vulva.
Lick lightly and kiss me your kudos.
Show devotion where devotion is due.

Here. Come.
Let me show you
my ovation face.

Objects in Mirror are Actually Pretty Far Away

Sure, I'd take another New Year's Eve
nuts deep in Jane, us laughing
at the fire hazard
of 32 lit candles in her
rat-trap apartment bedroom,

or a wine-soaked night
talking shit with
my wet finger cozy
in blind date Elise's
pink panties,

or a Sunday afternoon
drawing naked Nancy
and her silver-dollar nipples
on the carpeted floor
of a New Orleans double.

I would.
Of course, I would.

Seems all that mishegoss —
every kiss moan gasp —
should make more sense now.
Maybe not.
Probably not.

Is it wrong to want
to get up tomorrow
and not regret

a good call not made
or a bad call made,

that one party where the girl
who needed a ride home
didn't really
and boy I missed THAT boat
by a sea if not an ocean?

Well… fuck New Year's
in the ass with regrets.

I'm gonna wake the woman
who's in my bed right now
and lap at her cunt until
she bubbles like champagne.
I bet she can tell me my name.

another ball heard from

on the couch, we lurch toward midnight
both buzzed and bubbly both,
you smiling, shifting side-to-side
on your twice-shaved haunches,
amusedly anxious about sitting still
given where the champagne cork
has somehow found a niche.

we watch Ryan Seacrest dick about,
me already eager to greet the new year
with kisses at both your ends, finding and
pulling lightly at the jammed-up cork,
poking gently at your puffed-up jollies,
counting down how long I can twiddle
your revels 'til you pop.

lacuna

the threesome
    that-nearly wasn't
lingers,
its limbs
    longer in their absence,
its fingers
    missing from our skin,
its elbows
    never grazing mine or yours,
    never taking or adding
        weight to this bed,
this bed still wide enough
    for three,
again holding
    only two,
two mourning one
whose toothy grin
once ate S'mores
    and you
    in one night,
who twice
touched a spot
    you'd never found,
on whose ticklish belly
our hands once met —
    one going up,
    the other down.

Haiku VI

Aren't we the fine pair —
corset laced with silver thread,
your balls tied with gold?

∾

Snail on my nipple
undulates for attention.
Leaves a trail. "Call me."

∾

she finds unzipped
his eloquent erection
clear in its intent

∾

Asked what I desire,
I settle for the paddle,
still wanting the whip.

One button, then two.
It's incremental progress
that lets slip all things.

~

ropes creak supports hold
as she flies without a hitch
see what dangles down

~

Change hemispheres —
I love how she swirls her tongue
the opposite way.

~

how his cock catches
corona
look I got your nose

Like a Lion — or Maybe Showers

Even though there was
black ice on the driveway
just yesterday morning.

Even though there are
still snow mountains melting
in the mall parking lot.

Even though the trees
barely begin to bud
and the crocuses seem wary.

Even though the robin
in the backyard looks
both lost and lonely.

Even though the only
spring peeper I've heard
gave up and went back to sleep.

Even though all these things
suggest it's still winter,
I say it's spring.

Break out the May Pole!
Make cock rings from dandelions,
and slide with me into renewal.

Let's fuck against the nearest birch,
and make birds tilt their heads
and say, "Hell yeah!" when they hear you come.

Let's roll naked down grassy hills,
stay up to see the stars come out,
wake early to see the sunrise.

It's spring and I'm starving
either for rebirth or wet panties
pulled aside to let me in.

Spring is here! I tell you, it's true.
Rub against me, squirt across me,
ride me until we're raw and lobster red.

It's spring because I need a longer day
almost as much as I need you in short sleeves.
All the best flowers belong in their beds.

eat prey, love?

situationally-certain sidewinder
makes a tight dress, slit-skirt entrance,
zigzagging across the floor, angling

at something ahead, her directness
disguised by way of misdirection,
intent from door to bar, bar to me.

I watch how she flicks her pretty tongue
to strike fear in a swizzle stick
before baring teeth in a seeming smile.

tell me. am I to be sated hawk or fated mouse?
I worry we both lack the self-awareness
born of too much time on Tinder,

the good and common sense that might inform
which of us might choke on what we eat,
which of us might be easy to lick, hard to swallow.

As the Crow Flies

Desire is an impatient mistress, double-booked.
If you lived closer, ten miles instead of ten hundred,
would I hate each absence less and accept the delays

if I knew it takes less time, once the decision's made,
for you to find your way to me, toothbrush in hand,
with stories to tell and mischief on your mind?

Or is any time or distance short enough if tonight
I turn down the covers and don't see you waiting there,
tongue minty, toes waggling, panties tossed to the floor?

About the Writer

S.A. Harper has been writing dirty poems since high school. Those early poems were written in the style of long-dead Romantic, Cavalier, and metaphysical poets. Luckily, Harper's teachers could not bring themselves to complain about the passing references to thunderbolts or velvet purses. All things pass and, in college, Harper embraced free verse poetry and non-sequiturs. Bunnies.

This is S.A. Harper's third and possibly final collection of erotic poetry. 2025. Gotta love it.

Harper also writes erotic short stories. Those have more words and fewer line breaks than poems, but the body parts described and how those parts get used seem similar enough that Harper's stories might soon get the axe as well.

For other work by S.A. Harper,
please visit:

Word Oyster Press
wordoyster.com

You may contact the writer at:
saharper@wordoyster.com

www.ingramcontent.com/pod-product-compliance
Lightning Source LLC
Chambersburg PA
CBHW021209020426
42331CB00003B/276